# United States Presidents

# Chester Arthur

Paul Joseph
ABDO Publishing Company

# visit us at
# www.abdopub.com

Published by Abdo Publishing Company, 4940 Viking Drive, Edina, Minnesota 55435.
Copyright © 1999 by Abdo Consulting Group, Inc. International copyrights reserved in
all countries. No part of this book may be reproduced in any form without written
permission from the publisher.

Printed in the United States.

Cover and Interior Photo credits: AP/Wide World, Archive, Corbis-Bettmann

Contributing editors: Robert Italia, Tamara L. Britton, K. M. Brielmaier
Book design/maps: Patrick Laurel

## Library of Congress Cataloging-in-Publication Data

Joseph, Paul, 1970-
    Chester Arthur / Paul Joseph.
        p. cm. -- (United States presidents)
    Includes index.
    Summary: Discusses the personal life and brief political career of the lawyer
who became the twenty-first president of the United States in 1881.
    ISBN 1-57765-236-3
    1. Arthur, Chester Alan, 1829-1886--Juvenile literature. 2. Presidents--United
States --Biography--Juvenile literature. 3. Arthur, Chester Alan, 1829-1886. [1.
Presidents.] I. Title. II. Series: United States presidents (Edina, Minn.)
E692.J67   1999
973.8'4'092--dc21
    [B]                                                    98-16224
                                                            CIP
                                                            AC

3065200090 9889

# Contents

# Chester Arthur

*B*efore he was president, Chester Arthur worked as a New York City lawyer. Many people respected him. But Arthur had not worked much in politics.

Chester Arthur never held an elected office until he was vice president. **Republican** senators chose him for that job.

On September 19, 1881, Vice President Arthur was at home. There, he heard newsboys shouting, "President Garfield is dying!"

Around midnight, Vice President Arthur learned that Garfield had died. Arthur took the oath of office on September 20, 1881. Now, he was the twenty-first president. He worked hard and did a good job of leading America.

Throughout his life, Chester Arthur worked for the people. He was against slavery. And he fought for **civil rights**.

As a lawyer, Arthur helped an African American woman win a **lawsuit**. In another famous case, he helped a group of slaves win their freedom.

President Arthur fought dishonest government workers. He signed the first **civil service** law. And he rebuilt the U.S. Navy. These efforts helped Arthur win the nation's respect.

*Chester Arthur*

# *Chester Arthur* (1830-1886)
## Twenty-first President

| | |
|---|---|
| BORN: | October 5, 1830 |
| PLACE OF BIRTH: | Fairfield, Vermont |
| ANCESTRY: | Scots-Irish, English |
| FATHER: | William Arthur (1796-1875) |
| MOTHER: | Malvina Stone Arthur (1802-1869) |
| WIFE: | Ellen Lewis Herndon (1837-1880) |
| CHILDREN: | Three: 2 boys, 1 girl |
| EDUCATION: | Attended public schools and Lyceum School; Union College of Schenectady in 1848 |
| RELIGION: | Episcopalian |
| OCCUPATION: | Teacher, school principal, lawyer, customs official |
| MILITARY SERVICE: | Engineer-in-chief of New York troops during the Civil War; quartermaster general for New York State |
| POLITICAL PARTY: | Republican |

| | |
|---|---|
| OFFICES HELD: | Collector of customs, port of New York (1871-1878); vice president |
| AGE AT INAUGURATION: | 50 |
| YEARS SERVED: | 1881-1885 |
| VICE PRESIDENT: | None |
| DIED: | November 18, 1886, New York City, age 56 |
| CAUSE OF DEATH: | Stroke |

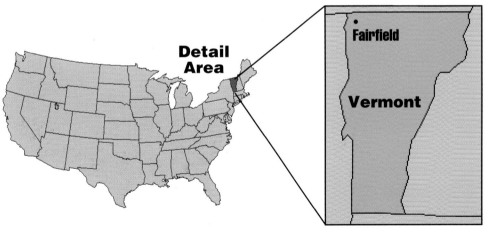

**Birthplace of Chester Arthur**

# Young Chester

*C*hester was born in Fairfield, Vermont, on October 5, 1830. His father, William Arthur, was a Baptist minister from Ireland. William moved to the United States when he was 18 years old.

Chester's mother, Malvina Stone Arthur, was from New Hampshire. Chester was the fifth of nine children. When Chester was nine, the family settled in Union Village, New York.

The Arthurs were a close and loving family. Both parents read, prayed, and educated their children. By age 15, Chester knew Latin and Greek.

Chester went to school in Union Village. He was an outstanding student. In 1844, the family moved to Schenectady, New York.

When Chester was 15 years old, he went to Union College. A year later, he had a part-time job teaching. In just three years, Chester graduated near the top of his class.

*The birthplace of Chester Arthur*

# Civil Rights Lawyer

$A$rthur's parents taught him to treat people with respect. His father spoke in church against slavery. Arthur wanted to do something to help African Americans.

Erastus D. Culver belonged to William Arthur's church. Culver was a **civil rights** lawyer. He thought Chester Arthur had the right ideas about people. In 1853, Arthur became Culver's **apprentice**.

Arthur helped Culver on the famous Lemmon Slave case. In 1852, Jonathan Lemmon brought eight slaves to New York from Virginia. New York state law did not allow slavery. The slaves wanted their freedom.

Lemmon refused to free them. The slaves did not live in New York, he said. So, the law did not apply to them. Judge Elijah Paine did not agree with Lemmon. The slaves were freed.

In 1854, Chester Arthur passed his law tests and became a lawyer. Culver saw many great things in Arthur. He worked hard, was smart, and loved his job. Arthur became a **partner** in Culver's law firm.

That year, Arthur defended African American Lizzie Jennings. She was forced off a streetcar reserved for white people. Arthur wanted a $500 judgment for Jennings. She was awarded $250.

The court victory helped change laws. Now, African Americans had the same rights as white passengers on streetcars.

Chester Arthur became famous around New York City. In 1856, Arthur started his own law practice.

*Chester Arthur as a civil rights lawyer*

# Family, Law, and Politics

*T*o get new business, Arthur joined clubs and entered politics. Arthur loved to talk about politics, books, and his favorite sport—fishing. He made many new friends. And his business grew.

Arthur also met Ellen Lewis Herndon. She was from Fredericksburg, Virginia. They married in 1859.

Chester and Ellen had three children. The first son, William Lewis, was born in 1860. He died when he was two. Chester Alan was born in 1864. Ellen Herndon was born in 1871. She was called Nell.

Arthur became more interested in politics. He helped form the new **Republican** party in New York State.

In 1860, New York governor Edwin D. Morgan, a Republican, was re-elected. The next year, he made Arthur the state engineer-in-chief.

In 1861, the **Civil War** began.  Arthur gave supplies to Union troops when they passed through New York City.

In 1862, Arthur became quartermaster general.  He oversaw **militia** groups.  And he helped prepare city defense plans.  He also made sure the state's forts and defenses were ready for war.

*Ellen Lewis Herndon Arthur*

# *The Making of the Twenty-first United States President*

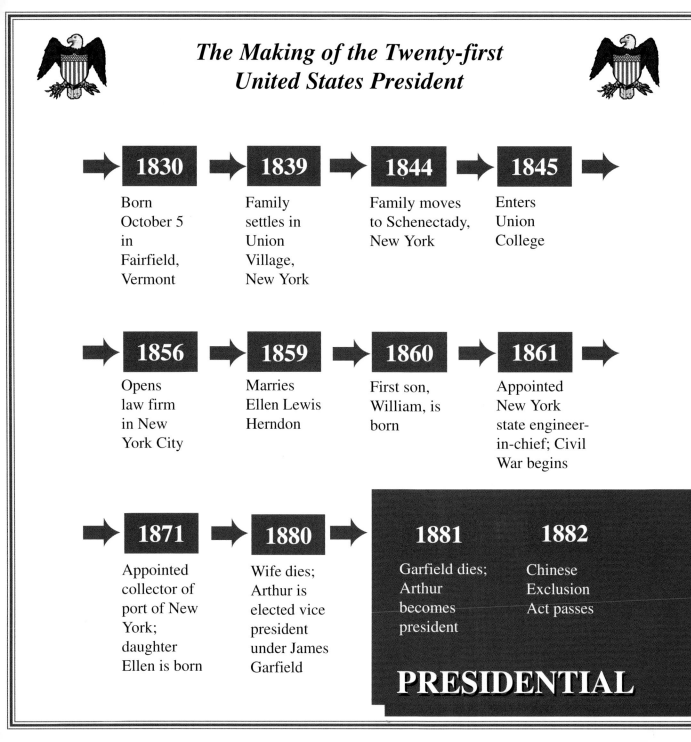

**1830**
Born
October 5
in
Fairfield,
Vermont

**1839**
Family
settles in
Union
Village,
New York

**1844**
Family moves
to Schenectady,
New York

**1845**
Enters
Union
College

**1856**
Opens
law firm
in New
York City

**1859**
Marries
Ellen Lewis
Herndon

**1860**
First son,
William, is
born

**1861**
Appointed
New York
state engineer-
in-chief; Civil
War begins

**1871**
Appointed
collector of
port of New
York;
daughter
Ellen is born

**1880**
Wife dies;
Arthur is
elected vice
president
under James
Garfield

**1881**
Garfield dies;
Arthur
becomes
president

**1882**
Chinese
Exclusion
Act passes

## PRESIDENTIAL

# Chester Arthur

*"No higher or more assuring proof could exist of the strength and permanence of popular government than the fact that though the chosen of the people be struck down, his constitutional successor is peacefully installed without shock or strain...."*

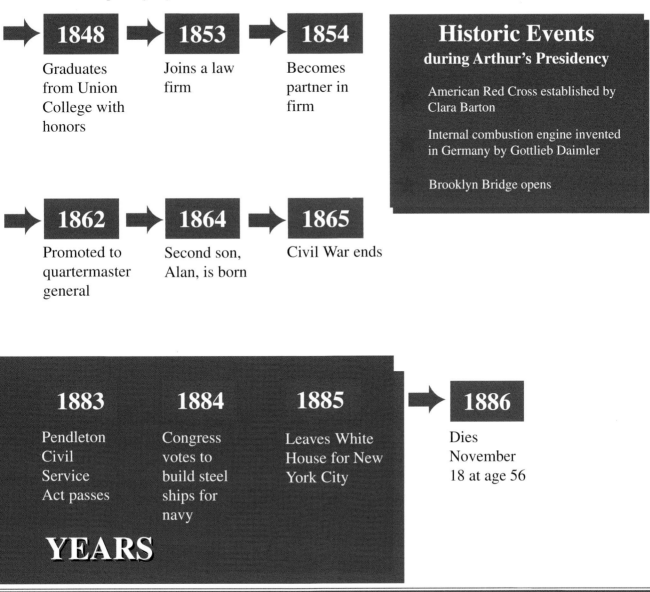

**1848**
Graduates from Union College with honors

**1853**
Joins a law firm

**1854**
Becomes partner in firm

## Historic Events
### during Arthur's Presidency

American Red Cross established by Clara Barton

Internal combustion engine invented in Germany by Gottlieb Daimler

Brooklyn Bridge opens

**1862**
Promoted to quartermaster general

**1864**
Second son, Alan, is born

**1865**
Civil War ends

**1883**
Pendleton Civil Service Act passes

**1884**
Congress votes to build steel ships for navy

**1885**
Leaves White House for New York City

**1886**
Dies November 18 at age 56

**YEARS**

# Working for the Government

*I*n 1863, a **Democrat** became governor of New York. Morgan and his staff—including Arthur—lost their jobs.

Arthur returned to his law practice. He got a lot of business. This made him a wealthy man.

In 1868, Arthur helped get Ulysses S. Grant elected president. Grant made Arthur the collector of the port of New York in 1871.

Arthur was in charge of the New York Customhouse. It collected much of the nation's **tariffs**. Arthur also managed 1,000 workers.

Arthur believed in the spoils system. He hired **Republicans** for key jobs in the Customhouse. In return, they had to give money to the Republican party. This gave the party a lot of money and power.

*President Ulysses S. Grant*

# Sad Days for
# Chester Arthur

*I*n 1877, Rutherford B. Hayes became U.S. president. Hayes did not like the spoils system. He felt that government jobs should be held by qualified people. Because Arthur believed in the spoils system, he lost his job.

Arthur was upset. He felt he had done a great job. Arthur returned to work as a lawyer. He also continued to help the **Republican** party.

In January 1880, Arthur was on a business trip. His wife became ill, so he rushed home. Ellen died of **pneumonia** on January 12. She was only 42.

Ellen had been a wonderful wife and mother. But Arthur neglected her during his political career. Still, Ellen never condemned him in public. Now, Arthur was sorry for his behavior.

Chester had to raise 16-year-old Alan and 9-year-old Nell alone. He had trouble working because of his wife's death. But he did the best he could.

*Nell Arthur, daughter of President Chester Arthur*

# The Twenty-first President

*I*n 1880, the **Republicans** chose James A. Garfield to run for president. They did not forget the work Arthur had done for the party. They picked him to run for vice president.

Garfield and Arthur won the election. Good luck returned to Arthur's life. On March 4, 1881, he became the nation's vice president.

Less than four months later, Charles Guiteau shot President Garfield. Guiteau was angry because Garfield wouldn't give him a job. For nearly two months, Garfield clung to life. On September 19, 1881, he died.

On September 20, 1881, Arthur took the oath of office in the living room of his New York home. Now, he was the twenty-first U.S. president.

Many Americans thought Arthur was unfit to be president. Outside New York State, people didn't know him. Arthur had never been an elected official. He had to win America's trust.

JAMES A. GARFIELD
REPUBLICAN CANDIDATE FOR PRESIDENT

CHESTER A. ARTHUR
REPUBLICAN CANDIDATE FOR VICE PRESIDENT

*Campaign poster from the election of 1880*

It wouldn't be easy. Arthur had Bright's disease. His kidneys weren't working correctly. He was always tired, and he had stomach problems. But he kept his illness a secret. Arthur didn't want people to think he was too sick to lead the nation.

Arthur took vacations so he could rest. While in Florida, Arthur caught **malaria**. This made him worse.

In 1883, Arthur signed the Pendleton Act—the nation's first **civil service** law. It required people to pass tests to get a government job. Americans liked this law. It is still in effect today.

Arthur also worked for the rights of Native Americans. He worked hard to protect their lands from settlers. And he believed they should have the same rights as everyone else.

President Arthur also improved the U.S. Navy. In 1884, he suggested a plan to replace wooden ships with steel ones. **Congress** approved the plan. For his efforts, Arthur is called the Father of the American Navy.

Existing
Territory

Existing
Territories

Existing
States

Existing States

**The
United States
in 1881**

# The Seven "Hats" of the U.S. President

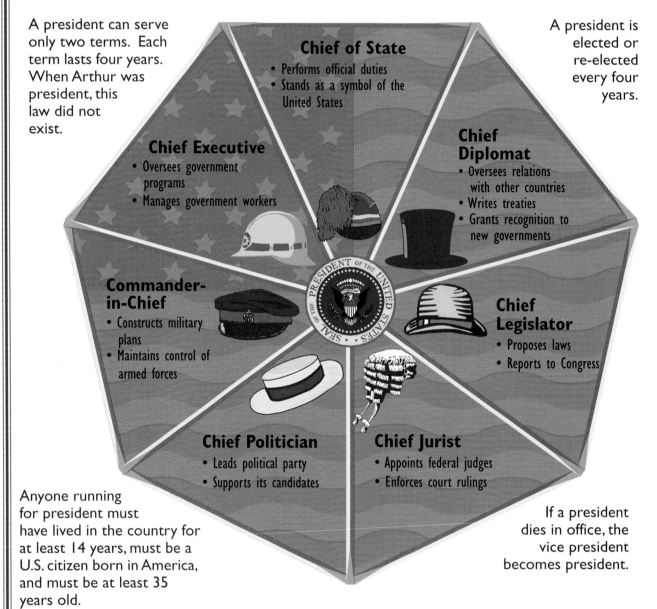

A president can serve only two terms. Each term lasts four years. When Arthur was president, this law did not exist.

A president is elected or re-elected every four years.

**Chief of State**
- Performs official duties
- Stands as a symbol of the United States

**Chief Executive**
- Oversees government programs
- Manages government workers

**Chief Diplomat**
- Oversees relations with other countries
- Writes treaties
- Grants recognition to new governments

**Commander-in-Chief**
- Constructs military plans
- Maintains control of armed forces

**Chief Legislator**
- Proposes laws
- Reports to Congress

**Chief Politician**
- Leads political party
- Supports its candidates

**Chief Jurist**
- Appoints federal judges
- Enforces court rulings

Anyone running for president must have lived in the country for at least 14 years, must be a U.S. citizen born in America, and must be at least 35 years old.

If a president dies in office, the vice president becomes president.

*As president, Chester Arthur had seven jobs.*

# The Three Branches of the U.S. Government

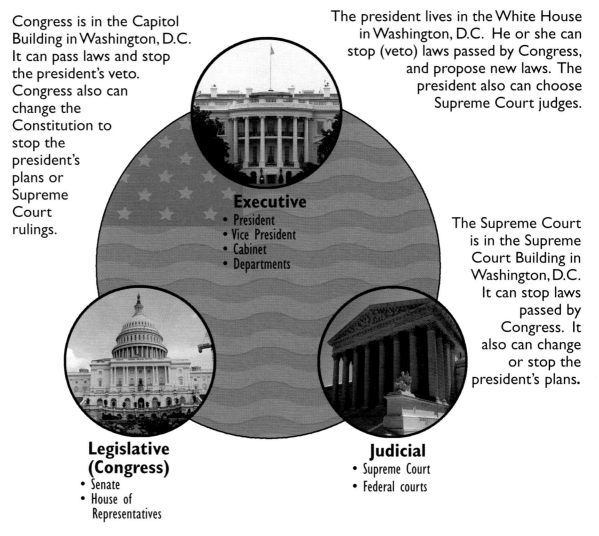

Congress is in the Capitol Building in Washington, D.C. It can pass laws and stop the president's veto. Congress also can change the Constitution to stop the president's plans or Supreme Court rulings.

The president lives in the White House in Washington, D.C. He or she can stop (veto) laws passed by Congress, and propose new laws. The president also can choose Supreme Court judges.

**Executive**
- President
- Vice President
- Cabinet
- Departments

The Supreme Court is in the Supreme Court Building in Washington, D.C. It can stop laws passed by Congress. It also can change or stop the president's plans.

**Legislative (Congress)**
- Senate
- House of Representatives

**Judicial**
- Supreme Court
- Federal courts

*The U.S. Constitution formed three government branches. Each branch has power over the others. So, no single group or person can control the country. The Constitution calls this "separation of powers."*

# Chester Arthur Goes Home

*C*hester Arthur loved to entertain in the White House. He enjoyed dances and fancy dinners. When dinner was over, he urged friends to stay. He disliked being alone. After they left, Arthur worked late into the night.

Arthur's sister, Mary Arthur McElroy, moved into the White House to keep him company. She also took care of Nell. By then, Alan was at the College of New Jersey. (It is now called Princeton University.)

President Arthur did what he thought was best for the country. But some of his ideas were not what the **Republicans** wanted. They did not choose him to run for re-election.

Chester Arthur accepted the party's decision. And he knew that he was too sick to be president again. He returned to his New York home on March 4, 1885.

Arthur tried to rebuild his law practice. But he lacked the energy. On November 18, 1886, Arthur died of a stroke. He was 56 years old.

Chester Alan Arthur will always be remembered as an honest man. He believed in the rights of all people. He worked hard at every job—especially as president of the United States.

*Chester Arthur enjoyed the outdoors.*

# Fun Facts

- When Chester Arthur became president, he refused to move into the White House until it had been cleaned and refurnished. Twenty-four wagon loads of rugs, furniture, and other belongings were carted off.

- President Arthur had a French chef in the White House. Many dinner parties lasted three or four hours.

- Chester Arthur loved flowers. He often had a flower in the buttonhole of his vest jacket. For one White House dinner, Arthur spent almost $1,500 on flowers. Most of his flowers came from New York.

- President Arthur's secretary of war was Robert Lincoln— President Abraham Lincoln's son.

- Chester Arthur was one of the finest fishermen in America. He once caught an 80-pound (36-kg) bass off the coast of Rhode Island.

*President Chester Arthur (standing in first boat) loved to fish.*

# Glossary

**apprentice** - a person who learns a trade or craft from a skilled worker.

**civil rights** - the rights of every U.S. citizen.

**civil service** - the part of the government that runs matters not covered by the military, the courts, or laws.

**Civil War** - a war between groups within the same country. The Northern and Southern states fought a civil war from 1861 to 1865 over slavery.

**Congress** - the lawmaking body of the U.S. It is made up of the Senate and the House of Representatives.

**Democrat** - one of the two main political parties in the U.S. Democrats are often liberal and believe in more government.

**lawsuit** - a court case started by a person claiming something from another.

**malaria** - a disease spread by mosquitoes that causes chills and fever.

**militia** - citizens trained for war or emergencies. The National Guard.

**partner** - one of two or more people who share a business.

**pneumonia** - a disease that causes difficult breathing and a high fever.

**Republican** - one of two main political parties in the United States. Republicans often are conservative and believe in less government.

**tariff** - fees or taxes placed on shipped goods.

# Internet Sites

**PBS American Presidents Series**
**http://www.americanpresidents.org**
Visit the PBS Web site which features the biographies of each president. Check out the key events of each presidency, speeches, fun facts, and trivia games.

**Welcome to the White House**
**http://www.whitehouse.gov**
The official Web site of the White House. After an introduction from the current president of the United States, the site takes you through biographies of each president. Get information on White House history, art in the White House, first ladies, first families, and much more.

**POTUS—Presidents of the United States**
**http://www.ipl.org/ref/POTUS/**
In this Web site you will find background information, election results, cabinet members, presidency highlights, and some odd facts on each of the presidents. Links to biographies, historical documents, audio and video files, and other presidential sites are also included to enrich this site.

*These sites are subject to change. Go to your favorite search engine and type in United States presidents for more sites.*

# Pass It On

  History enthusiasts: educate readers around the country by passing on information you've learned about presidents or other important people who have changed history. Share your little-known facts and interesting stories. We want to hear from you!

**To get posted on the ABDO Publishing Company Web site, email us at "History@abdopub.com"**
**Visit the ABDO Publishing Company Web site at www.abdopub.com**

# Index

| DATE | | | |
|---|---|---|---|
| | | | |
| | | | |
| | | | |
| | | | |
| | | | |
| | | | |
| | | | |
| | | | |
| | | | |
| | | | |
| | | | |
| | | | |
| | | | |